a·ZOO·for·YOU

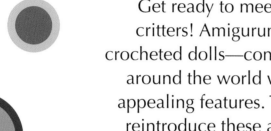

Get ready to meet some incredibly cute critters! Amigurumi—the Japanese art of crocheted dolls—continues to charm crocheters around the world with their small size and appealing features. That's why we decided to reintroduce these adorable zoo animals by Cindy Harris. The little figures are so quick and fun to make, you may be tempted to crochet the entire collection for yourself, your friends, and all the youngsters you know!

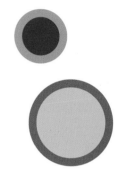

LEISURE ARTS, INC.
Little Rock, Arkansas

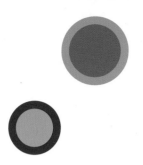

• MATERIALS •

- Medium Weight Yarn:
  See Individual designs for yardages
- Crochet hook, size F (3.75 mm)
- Polyester stuffing
- Yarn needle
- Finishing materials: Moveable eyes, embroidery floss, and glue

■■□□ **EASY**

Note: If toy is intended for children under 3 years old, we recommend embroidering the eyes.

• •

• MONKEY •

Black - 20 yards (18.5 meters)
Tan - 2 yards (1.8 meters)

HEAD AND BODY

With Black, ch 3 **loosely**; being careful not to twist ch, join with slip st to form a ring.

Rnd 1 (Right side): Ch 1, 2 sc in each ch around; do **not** join, place marker *(see Markers, page 15)*: 6 sc.

Rnd 2: 2 Sc in each sc around: 12 sc.

Rnds 3-5: Sc in each sc around.

Stuff firmly.

Rnd 6: Decrease around *(see Decrease, page 15)*: 6 sc.

Rnd 7: Sc in each sc around.

Rnd 8: 2 Sc in each sc around: 12 sc.

Rnds 9-13: Sc in each sc around.

Stuff firmly.

Rnd 14: Decrease around: 6 sc.

Rnd 15: (Skip next sc, slip st in next sc) around; finish off.

EAR (Make 2)

Row 1 (Right side): With Black, ch 2, 3 sc in second ch from hook; finish off leaving a long end for sewing.

Sew Ears to Head.

MUZZLE

Rnd 1 (Right side): With Tan, ch 4 **loosely**; 2 sc in second ch from hook, sc in next ch, 4 sc in last ch; working in free loops of beginning ch *(Fig. 3b, page 15)*, sc in next ch, 2 sc in next ch; join with slip st to first sc, finish off leaving a long end for sewing.

Sew Muzzle to Head.

LIMB (Make 2 for Legs & 2 for Arms)

Row 1 (Right side): With Black, ch 11 **loosely**; dc in third ch from hook and in each ch across; finish off leaving a long end for sewing.

With **right** side to inside, fold lengthwise. Working through free loops of beginning ch and both loops of each dc, sew across.

Sew Legs to Body, curving inward; then sew Arms to Body, curving upward.

TAIL

Row 1: With Black, ch 19 **loosely**; slip st in second ch from hook and in each ch across; finish off leaving a long end for sewing.

Sew Tail to Body.

Add features as desired. •

• BROWN BEAR •
Brown - 35 yards (32 meters)
Tan - 5 yards (4.6 meters)

BODY
With Brown, ch 3 **loosely**; being careful not to twist ch, join with slip st to form a ring.

Rnd 1 (Right side): Ch 1, 2 sc in each ch around; do **not** join, place marker *(see Markers, page 15)*: 6 sc.

Rnd 2: 2 Sc in each sc around: 12 sc.

Rnd 3: (Sc in next sc, 2 sc in next sc) around: 18 sc.

Rnds 4-10: Sc in each sc around.

Rnd 11: ★ Sc in next sc, decrease *(see Decrease, page 15)*; repeat from ★ around: 12 sc.

Stuff firmly.

Rnd 12: Decrease around: 6 sc.

Rnd 13: (Skip next sc, slip st in next sc) around; finish off.

HEAD
With Brown, ch 3 **loosely**; being careful not to twist ch, join with slip st to form a ring.

Rnd 1 (Right side): Ch 1, 2 sc in each ch around; do **not** join, place marker: 6 sc.

Rnd 2: 2 Sc in each sc around: 12 sc.

Rnd 3: (Sc in next sc, 2 sc in next sc) around: 18 sc.

Rnds 4-6: Sc in each sc around.

Rnd 7: Decrease around; slip st in next sc, finish off leaving a long end for sewing.

Stuff firmly and sew Head to Body.

EAR (Make 2)
With Brown, ch 3 **loosely**; being careful not to twist ch, join with slip st to form a ring.

Rnd 1 (Right side): Ch 1, 2 sc in each ch around; join with slip st to first sc, finish off leaving a long end for sewing.

Sew Ears to Head.

MUZZLE
With Tan, ch 3 **loosely**; being careful not to twist ch, join with slip st to form a ring.

Rnd 1 (Right side): Ch 1, 2 sc in each ch around; do **not** join, place marker: 6 sc.

Rnd 2: (Sc in next sc, 2 sc in next sc) around; slip st in next sc, finish off leaving a long end for sewing.

Stuff lightly and sew Muzzle to Head.

LEG (Make 4)
With Brown, ch 3 **loosely**; being careful not to twist ch, join with slip st to form a ring.

Rnd 1 (Right side): Ch 1, 2 sc in each ch around; do **not** join, place marker: 6 sc.

Rnd 2: 2 Sc in each sc around: 12 sc.

Rnd 3: Decrease 3 times, sc in next 6 sc: 9 sc.

Rnds 4-8: Sc in each sc around; at end of Rnd 8, slip st in next sc, finish off leaving a long end for sewing.

Stuff firmly and sew Legs to Body.

TAIL
With Brown, ch 3 **loosely**; being careful not to twist ch, join with slip st to form a ring.

Rnd 1 (Right side): Ch 1, 2 sc in each ch around; do **not** join, place marker: 6 sc.

Rnd 2: Sc in each sc around; slip st in next sc, finish off leaving a long end for sewing.

Stuff lightly and sew Tail to Body.

Add features as desired. •

• HIPPO •
Grey - 48 yards (44 meters)

BODY
With Grey, ch 3 **loosely**; being careful not to twist ch, join with slip st to form a ring.

Rnd 1 (Right side)**:** Ch 1, 2 sc in each ch around; do **not** join, place marker **(see Markers, page 15)**: 6 sc.

Rnd 2: 2 Sc in each sc around: 12 sc.

Rnd 3: (Sc in next sc, 2 sc in next sc) around: 18 sc.

Rnd 4: (Sc in next 5 sc, 2 sc in next sc) around: 21 sc.

Rnds 5-13: Sc in each sc around.

Rnd 14: ★ Sc in next 5 sc, decrease **(see Decrease, page 15)**; repeat from ★ around: 18 sc.

Rnd 15: (Sc in next sc, decrease) around: 12 sc.

Stuff firmly.

Rnd 16: Decrease around: 6 sc.

Rnd 17: (Skip next sc, slip st in next sc) around; finish off.

HEAD
With Grey, ch 5 **loosely**.

Rnd 1 (Right side)**:** 2 Sc in second ch from hook, sc in next 2 chs, 4 sc in last ch; working in free loops of beginning ch **(Fig. 3b, page 15)**, sc in next 2 chs, 2 sc in next ch; do **not** join, place marker: 12 sc.

Rnd 2: (Sc in next sc, 2 sc in next sc) around: 18 sc.

Rnd 3: (Sc in next 2 sc, 2 sc in next sc) around: 24 sc.

Rnd 4: Sc in each sc around.

Rnd 5: (Sc in next 6 sc, decrease) around: 21 sc.

Rnd 6: (Sc in next 5 sc, decrease) around: 18 sc.

Rnd 7: (Sc in next 4 sc, decrease) around: 15 sc.

Rnd 8: Sc in each sc around.

Rnd 9: (Sc in next 4 sc, 2 sc in next sc) around: 18 sc.

Rnds 10 and 11: Sc in each sc around.

Rnd 12: (Sc in next sc, decrease) around: 12 sc.

Stuff firmly.

Rnd 13: Decrease around: 6 sc.

Rnd 14: (Skip next sc, slip st in next sc) around; finish off.

Sew Head to Body.

EAR (Make 2)
Row 1 (Right side)**:** With Grey, ch 2, (2 sc, slip st) in second ch from hook; finish off leaving a long end for sewing.

Sew Ears to Head.

LEG (Make 4)
With Grey, ch 3 **loosely**; being careful not to twist ch, join with slip st to form a ring.

Rnd 1 (Right side)**:** Ch 1, 2 sc in each ch around; do **not** join, place marker: 6 sc.

Rnd 2: 2 Sc in each sc around: 12 sc.

Rnds 3-5: Sc in each sc around; at end of Rnd 5, slip st in next sc, finish off leaving a long end for sewing.

Stuff firmly and sew Legs to Body.

TAIL
Row 1: With Grey, ch 6 **loosely**; slip st in second ch from hook and in each ch across; finish off leaving a long end for sewing.

Sew Tail to Body.

Add features as desired. •

• TIGER •

Orange - 28 yards (25.5 meters)
Black - 4 yards (3.7 meters)

BODY

With Orange, ch 3 **loosely**; being careful not to twist ch, join with slip st to form a ring.

Rnd 1 (Right side)**:** Ch 1, 2 sc in each ch around; do **not** join, place marker *(see Markers, page 15)*: 6 sc.

Rnd 2: 2 Sc in each sc around: 12 sc.

Rnd 3: (Sc in next 2 sc, 2 sc in next sc) around: 16 sc.

Rnds 4-11: Sc in each sc around.

Rnd 12: ★ Sc in next 2 sc, decrease *(see Decrease, page 15)*; repeat from ★ around: 12 sc.

Stuff firmly.

Rnd 13: Decrease around: 6 sc.

Rnd 14: (Skip next sc, slip st in next sc) around; finish off.

HEAD

With Orange, ch 3 **loosely**; being careful not to twist ch, join with slip st to form a ring.

Rnd 1 (Right side)**:** Ch 1, 2 sc in each ch around; do **not** join, place marker: 6 sc.

Rnd 2: 2 Sc in each sc around: 12 sc.

Rnd 3: (Sc in next 2 sc, 2 sc in next sc) around: 16 sc.

Rnds 4-6: Sc in each sc around.

Rnd 7: Decrease around: 8 sc.

Rnds 8 and 9: Sc in each sc around; at end of Rnd 9, slip st in next sc, finish off leaving a long end for sewing.

Stuff firmly and sew Head to Body.

EAR (Make 2)

Row 1 (Right side)**:** With Orange, ch 2, 4 sc in second ch from hook; finish off leaving a long end for sewing.

Sew Ears to Head.

CHEEK (Make 2)

With Orange, ch 3 **loosely**; being careful not to twist ch, join with slip st to form a ring.

Rnd 1 (Right side)**:** Ch 1, 2 sc in each ch around; join with slip st to first sc, finish off leaving a long end for sewing.

Sew Cheeks to Head.

LEG (Make 4)

With Orange, ch 3 **loosely**; being careful not to twist ch, join with slip st to form a ring.

Rnd 1 (Right side)**:** Ch 1, 2 sc in each ch around; do **not** join, place marker: 6 sc.

Note: Every few rounds, stuff firmly.

Rnd 2: 2 Sc in each of next 2 sc, sc in next 4 sc: 8 sc.

Rnd 3: Decrease twice, sc in next 4 sc: 6 sc.

Rnds 4-7: Sc in each sc around.

Rnd 8: (Sc in next 2 sc, 2 sc in next sc) twice; slip st in next sc, finish off leaving a long end for sewing.

Sew Legs to Body.

TAIL

Rnd 1 (Right side)**:** With Orange, ch 2, 4 sc in second ch from hook; do **not** join, place marker.

Note: Tail is **not** stuffed.

Rnds 2-16: Sc in each sc around; at end of Rnd 16, slip st in next sc, finish off leaving a long end for sewing.

Sew Tail to Body.

With Black, add stripes.

Add features as desired. •

• RHINO •
Grey - 40 yards (36.5 meters)

HEAD AND BODY
With Grey, ch 3 **loosely**; being careful not to twist ch, join with slip st to form a ring.

Rnd 1 (Right side): Ch 1, 2 sc in each ch around; do **not** join, place marker *(see Markers, page 15)*: 6 sc.

Rnd 2: (Sc in next sc, 2 sc in next sc) around: 9 sc.

Rnd 3: (Sc in next 2 sc, 2 sc in next sc) around: 12 sc.

Rnds 4 and 5: Sc in each sc around.

Rnd 6: 2 Sc in each of next 4 sc (forehead), sc in next 8 sc: 16 sc.

Rnds 7-10: Sc in each sc around.

Rnd 11: ★ Sc in next 2 sc, decrease *(see Decrease, page 15)*; repeat from ★ around: 12 sc.

Rnd 12: Sc in each sc around.

Rnd 13: (Sc in next sc, 2 sc in next sc) around: 18 sc.

Rnd 14: (Sc in next 2 sc, 2 sc in next sc) around: 24 sc.

Rnds 15-24: Sc in each sc around.

Rnd 25: (Sc in next 2 sc, decrease) around: 18 sc.

Rnd 26: (Sc in next sc, decrease) around: 12 sc.

Stuff firmly.

Rnd 27: Decrease around: 6 sc.

Rnd 28: (Skip next sc, slip st in next sc) around; finish off.

EAR (Make 2)
Row 1 (Right side): With Grey, ch 4 **loosely**; slip st in second ch from hook, sc in next ch, slip st in last ch; finish off leaving a long end for sewing.

Sew Ears to Head.

HORNS
SMALL
Rnd 1 (Right side): With Grey, ch 2, 4 sc in second ch from hook; do **not** join, place marker.

Rnd 2: Sc in each sc around; slip st in next sc, finish off leaving a long end for sewing.

Sew Small Horn to Head just below forehead.

LARGE
Rnd 1 (Right side): With Grey, ch 2, 4 sc in second ch from hook; do **not** join, place marker.

Rnd 2: Sc in each sc around.

Rnd 3: (Sc in next sc, 2 sc in next sc) twice: 6 sc.

Rnd 4: Sc in each sc around; slip st in next sc, finish off leaving a long end for sewing.

Stuff firmly and sew Large Horn to Head in front of Small Horn.

LEG (Make 4)
With Grey, ch 3 **loosely**; being careful not to twist ch, join with slip st to form a ring.

Rnd 1 (Right side): Ch 1, 2 sc in each ch around; do **not** join, place marker: 6 sc.

Rnd 2: 2 Sc in each sc around: 12 sc.

Rnds 3-6: Sc in each sc around; at end of Rnd 6, slip st in next sc, finish off leaving a long end for sewing.

Stuff firmly and sew Legs to Body.

TAIL
Row 1: With Grey, ch 4 **loosely**; slip st in second ch from hook and in each ch across; finish off leaving a long end for sewing.

Sew Tail to Body.

Cut two 8" (20.5 cm) strands of Grey. Hold strands together and draw through slip st at end of Tail; tie ends in a knot. Trim as desired.

Add features as desired. •

• GIRAFFE •
Gold - 48 yards (44 meters)
Brown - 10 yards (9 meters)

BODY
With Gold, ch 3 **loosely**; being careful not to twist ch, join with slip st to form a ring.

Rnd 1 (Right side): Ch 1, 2 sc in each ch around; do **not** join, place marker *(see Markers, page 15)*: 6 sc.

Rnd 2: 2 Sc in each sc around: 12 sc.

Rnd 3: (Sc in next 2 sc, 2 sc in next sc) around: 16 sc.

Rnds 4-12: Sc in each sc around.

Rnd 13: ★ Sc in next 2 sc, decrease *(see Decrease, page 15)*; repeat from ★ around: 12 sc.

Stuff firmly.

Rnd 14: Decrease around: 6 sc.

Rnd 15: (Skip next sc, slip st in next sc) around; finish off.

HEAD AND NECK
With Gold, ch 3 **loosely**; being careful not to twist ch, join with slip st to form a ring.

Rnd 1 (Right side): Ch 1, 2 sc in each ch around; do **not** join, place marker: 6 sc.

Note: Every few rounds, stuff firmly.

Rnd 2: 2 Sc in each sc around: 12 sc.

Rnd 3: (Sc in next 2 sc, 2 sc in next sc) around: 16 sc.

Rnds 4-6: Sc in each sc around.

Rnd 7: Decrease around: 8 sc.

Rnds 8-17: Sc in each sc around; at end of Rnd 17, slip st in next sc, finish off leaving a long end for sewing.

Sew Neck to Body.

EAR (Make 2)
Row 1 (Right side): With Gold, ch 4 **loosely**; sc in second ch from hook and in next ch, slip st in last ch; finish off leaving a long end for sewing.

Sew Ears to Head.

MUZZLE
With Gold, ch 3 **loosely**; being careful not to twist ch, join with slip st to form a ring.

Rnd 1 (Right side): Ch 1, 2 sc in each ch around; do **not** join, place marker: 6 sc.

Rnd 2: (Sc in next sc, 2 sc in next sc) around: 9 sc.

Rnd 3: Sc in each sc around; slip st in next sc, finish off leaving a long end for sewing.

Stuff lightly and sew Muzzle to Head.

HORN (Make 2)
Row 1 (Right side): With Brown, ch 3 **loosely**; 3 sc in second ch from hook, slip st in last ch; finish off leaving a long end for sewing.

Sew Horns to Head.

LEG (Make 4)
With Brown, ch 3 **loosely**; being careful not to twist ch, join with slip st to form a ring.

Rnd 1 (Right side): Ch 1, 2 sc in each ch around; do **not** join, place marker: 6 sc.

Note: Every few rounds, stuff firmly.

Rnd 2: (Sc in next 2 sc, 2 sc in next sc) twice changing to Gold in last sc *(Fig. 1, page 15)*: 8 sc.

Rnds 3-14: Sc in each sc around; at end of Rnd 14, slip st in next sc, finish off leaving a long end for sewing.

Sew Legs to Body.

TAIL
Row 1: With Gold, ch 8 **loosely**; slip st in second ch from hook and in each ch across; finish off leaving a long end for sewing.

Sew Tail to Body.

Cut two 8" (20.5 cm) strands of Brown. Hold strands together and draw through slip st at end of Tail; tie ends in a knot. Trim as desired.

With Brown, add spots.

Add features as desired. •

• POLAR BEAR •

White - 23 yards (21 meters)

BODY

With White, ch 3 **loosely**; being careful not to twist ch, join with slip st to form a ring.

Rnd 1 (Right side)**:** Ch 1, 2 sc in each ch around; do **not** join, place marker *(see Markers, page 15)*: 6 sc.

Rnd 2: 2 Sc in each sc around: 12 sc.

Rnd 3: (Sc in next 2 sc, 2 sc in next sc) around: 16 sc.

Rnds 4-10: Sc in each sc around.

Rnd 11: Decrease around *(see Decrease, page 15)*: 8 sc.

Stuff firmly.

Rnd 12: Decrease around: 4 sc.

Rnd 13: (Skip next sc, slip st in next sc) twice; finish off.

HEAD

With White, ch 3 **loosely**; being careful not to twist ch, join with slip st to form a ring.

Rnd 1 (Right side)**:** Ch 1, 2 sc in each ch around; do **not** join, place marker: 6 sc.

Rnd 2: (Sc in next 2 sc, 2 sc in next sc) twice: 8 sc.

Rnd 3: (Sc in next 3 sc, 2 sc in next sc) twice: 10 sc.

Rnd 4: (Sc in next 4 sc, 2 sc in next sc) twice: 12 sc.

Rnd 5: (Sc in next 3 sc, 2 sc in next sc) around: 15 sc.

Rnd 6: Sc in each sc around.

Rnd 7: (Sc in next 3 sc, decrease) around: 12 sc.

Stuff firmly.

Rnd 8: Decrease around: 6 sc.

Rnd 9: (Skip next sc, slip st in next sc) around; finish off.

Sew Head to Body.

EAR (Make 2)

Row 1 (Right side)**:** With White, ch 2, (2 sc, slip st) in second ch from hook; finish off leaving a long end for sewing.

Sew Ears to Head.

BACK LEG (Make 2)

With White, ch 3 **loosely**; being careful not to twist ch, join with slip st to form a ring.

Rnd 1 (Right side)**:** Ch 1, 2 sc in each ch around; do **not** join, place marker: 6 sc.

Rnd 2: 2 Sc in each sc around: 12 sc.

Rnd 3: Decrease 4 times, sc in next 4 sc: 8 sc.

Rnds 4-6: Sc in each sc around.

Rnd 7: (Sc in next 3 sc, 2 sc in next sc) twice; slip st in next sc, finish off leaving a long end for sewing.

Stuff firmly and sew Back Legs to Body.

FRONT LEG (Make 2)

With White, ch 3 **loosely**; being careful not to twist ch, join with slip st to form a ring.

Rnd 1 (Right side)**:** Ch 1, 2 sc in each ch around; do **not** join, place marker: 6 sc.

Rnd 2: (Sc in next 2 sc, 2 sc in next sc) twice: 8 sc.

Rnds 3-6: Sc in each sc around.

Note: Begin working in rows.

Row 1: Sc in next 6 sc, leave remaining 2 sc unworked.

Row 2: Ch 1, turn; decrease, sc in next 2 sc, decrease: 4 sc.

Row 3: Ch 1, turn; decrease twice; finish off leaving a long end for sewing.

Stuff firmly and sew Front Legs to Body.

TAIL

With White, ch 3 **loosely**; being careful not to twist ch, join with slip st to form a ring.

Rnd 1 (Right side)**:** Ch 1, 2 sc in each ch around; do **not** join, place marker: 6 sc.

Rnd 2: (Sc in next 2 sc, 2 sc in next sc) twice: 8 sc.

Rnd 3: (Sc in next 2 sc, decrease) twice; slip st in next sc, finish off leaving a long end for sewing.

Stuff lightly and sew Tail to Body.

Add features as desired.•

• LION •

Lt Orange - 32 yards (29.5 meters)
Rust and Brown - 5 yards (4.6 meters) **each** color

BODY
With Lt Orange, ch 3 **loosely**; being careful not to twist ch, join with slip st to form a ring.

Rnd 1 (Right side)**:** Ch 1, 2 sc in each ch around; do **not** join, place marker **(see Markers, page 15)**: 6 sc.

Rnd 2: 2 Sc in each sc around: 12 sc.

Rnd 3: (Sc in next sc, 2 sc in next sc) around: 18 sc.

Rnds 4-12: Sc in each sc around.

Rnd 13: ★ Sc in next sc, decrease **(see Decrease, page 15)**; repeat from ★ around: 12 sc.

Stuff firmly.

Rnd 14: Decrease around: 6 sc.

Rnd 15: (Skip next sc, slip st in next sc) around; finish off.

HEAD
With Lt Orange, ch 3 **loosely**; being careful not to twist ch, join with slip st to form a ring.

Rnd 1 (Right side)**:** Ch 1, 2 sc in each ch around; do **not** join, place marker: 6 sc.

Rnd 2: 2 Sc in each sc around: 12 sc.

Rnd 3: (Sc in next 2 sc, 2 sc in next sc) around: 16 sc.

Rnd 4: Sc in each sc around; slip st in Back Loop Only of next sc **(Fig. 2, page 15)**.

Rnd 5: Ch 1, sc in Back Loop Only of same st and each sc around.

Rnd 6: Sc in Back Loop Only of each sc around.

Rnd 7: Working in Back Loops Only, decrease around: 8 sc.

Rnds 8 and 9: Sc in both loops of each sc around; at end of Rnd 9, slip st in next sc, finish off leaving a long end for sewing.

Stuff firmly and sew Head to Body.

EAR (Make 2)
Row 1 (Right side)**:** With Lt Orange, ch 2, 4 sc in second ch from hook; finish off leaving a long end for sewing.

Sew Ears to Head.

CHEEK (Make 2)
With Lt Orange, ch 3 **loosely**; being careful not to twist ch, join with slip st to form a ring.

Rnd 1 (Right side)**:** Ch 1, 2 sc in each ch around; join with slip st to first sc, finish off leaving a long end for sewing.

Sew Cheeks to Head.

LEG (Make 4)
With Lt Orange, ch 3 **loosely**; being careful not to twist ch, join with slip st to form a ring.

Rnd 1 (Right side)**:** Ch 1, 2 sc in each ch around; do **not** join, place marker: 6 sc.

Rnd 2: 2 Sc in each sc around: 12 sc.

Rnd 3: Decrease 4 times, sc in next 4 sc: 8 sc.

Rnds 4-8: Sc in each sc around; at end of Rnd 8, slip st in next sc, finish off leaving a long end for sewing.

Stuff firmly and sew Legs to Body.

TAIL
Row 1: With Lt Orange, ch 19 **loosely**; slip st in second ch from hook and in each ch across; finish off leaving a long end for sewing.

Sew Tail to Body.

Cut one 8" (20.5 cm) strand **each** of Rust, Brown, and Lt Orange. Hold strands together and draw through slip st at end of Tail; tie ends in a knot. Trim as desired.

MANE
Cut forty-eight 3" (7.5 cm) strands **each** of Rust, Brown, and Lt Orange.

Hold one strand of each color together and fold in half. With Body toward you, insert crochet hook in free loop on Head **(Fig. 3a, page 15)** and draw the folded end through the free loop. Pull the loose ends through the folded end; draw the knot up **tightly**. Repeat in **each** remaining free loop. Trim as desired.

Add features as desired.•

• ZEBRA •
Black - 33 yards (30 meters)
White - 25 yards (23 meters)

BODY
With Black, ch 3 **loosely**; being careful not to twist ch, join with slip st to form a ring.

Rnd 1 (Right side)**:** Ch 1, 2 sc in each ch around changing to White in last sc *(Fig. 1, page 15)*; do **not** join, place marker *(see Markers, page 15)*: 6 sc.

Note: Change colors in last stitch of each round, alternating Black and White and carrying yarn **loosely** along **wrong** side. Do **not** cut yarn unless otherwise specified.

Rnd 2: 2 Sc in each sc around: 12 sc.

Rnd 3: (Sc in next 3 sc, 2 sc in next sc) around: 15 sc.

Rnds 4-13: Sc in each sc around.

Rnd 14: ★ Sc in next 3 sc, decrease *(see Decrease, page 15)*; repeat from ★ around, cut White: 12 sc.

Stuff firmly.

Rnd 15: Decrease around: 6 sc.

Rnd 16: (Skip next sc, slip st in next sc) around; finish off.

HEAD
With Black, ch 3 **loosely**; being careful not to twist ch, join with slip st to form a ring.

Rnd 1 (Right side)**:** Ch 1, 2 sc in each ch around; do **not** join, place marker: 6 sc.

Rnd 2: (Sc in next 2 sc, 2 sc in next sc) twice changing to White in last sc: 8 sc.

Note: Change colors in last stitch of each round, alternating Black and White and carrying yarn **loosely** along **wrong** side. Do **not** cut yarn unless otherwise specified.

Rnds 3 and 4: Sc in each sc around.

Rnd 5: (Sc in next 3 sc, 2 sc in next sc) twice: 10 sc.

Rnd 6: (Sc in next 4 sc, 2 sc in next sc) twice: 12 sc.

Rnd 7: Sc in each sc around.

Rnd 8: (Sc in next 2 sc, 2 sc in next sc) around: 16 sc.

Rnd 9: Sc in each sc around.

Stuff firmly.

Rnds 10 and 11: Decrease around; at end of Rnd 10, cut Black: 4 sc.

Rnd 12: (Skip next sc, slip st in next sc) twice; finish off.

NECK
With White and leaving a long end for sewing, ch 10 **loosely**; being careful not to twist ch, join with slip st to form a ring changing to Black.

Rnd 1 (Right side)**:** Ch 1, sc in each ch around changing to White in last sc; do **not** join, place marker, do **not** finish off: 10 sc.

Note: Change colors in last stitch of each round, alternating Black and White and carrying yarn **loosely** along **wrong** side. Do **not** cut yarn unless otherwise specified.

Rnd 2: (Sc in next 4 sc, 2 sc in next sc) twice: 12 sc.

Rnd 3: Sc in each sc around, cut Black.

Rnd 4: Sc in each sc around; slip st in next sc, finish off leaving a long end for sewing.

Sew Rnd 1 of Neck to Head.

Stuff firmly and sew Rnd 4 of Neck to Body.

EAR (Make 2)
Row 1 (Right side)**:** With Black, ch 3 **loosely**; slip st in second ch from hook, sc in last ch; finish off leaving a long end for sewing.

Sew Ears to Head.

LEG (Make 4)

With Black, ch 3 **loosely**; being careful not to twist ch, join with slip st to form a ring.

Rnd 1 (Right side): Ch 1, 2 sc in each ch around; do **not** join, place marker: 6 sc.

Note: Every few rounds, stuff firmly.

Rnd 2: Sc in each sc around changing to White in last sc.

Note: Change colors in last stitch of each round, alternating Black and White and carrying yarn **loosely** along **wrong** side. Do **not** cut yarn unless otherwise specified.

Rnds 3-5: Sc in each sc around.

Rnd 6: (Sc in next sc, 2 sc in next sc) around: 9 sc.

Rnd 7: Sc in each sc around.

Rnd 8: (Sc in next sc, decrease) around: 6 sc.

Rnds 9-11: Sc in each sc around.

Rnd 12: (Sc in next 2 sc, 2 sc in next sc) twice; cut Black: 8 sc.

Rnd 13: (Sc in next 3 sc, 2 sc in next sc) twice; slip st in next sc, finish off leaving a long end for sewing.

Sew Legs to Body.

TAIL

Row 1: With Black, ch 5 **loosely**; slip st in second ch from hook and in each ch across; finish off leaving a long end for sewing.

Sew Tail to Body.

Cut two 8" (20.5 cm) strands of Black and one 8" (20.5 cm) strand of White. Hold strands together and draw through slip st at end of Tail; tie ends in a knot. Trim as desired.

MANE

★ Cut seven 3" (7.5 cm) strands of Black; hold strands together and tie in center with a 10" (25.5 cm) strand of Black to form a portion of Mane. Using long ends, attach to Head.

Repeat from ★ to form entire Mane. Trim as desired.

Add features as desired. ▪

• ELEPHANT •
Lt Grey - 80 yards (73 meters)

BODY

With Lt Grey, ch 3 **loosely**; being careful not to twist ch, join with slip st to form a ring.

Rnd 1 (Right side): Ch 1, 2 sc in each ch around; do **not** join, place marker *(see Markers, page 15)*: 6 sc.

Rnd 2: 2 Sc in each sc around: 12 sc.

Rnd 3: (Sc in next sc, 2 sc in next sc) around: 18 sc.

Rnd 4: (Sc in next 2 sc, 2 sc in next sc) around: 24 sc.

Rnds 5-15: Sc in each sc around.

Rnd 16: ★ Sc in next 2 sc, decrease *(see Decrease, page 15)*; repeat from ★ around: 18 sc.

Rnd 17: (Sc in next sc, decrease) around: 12 sc.

Stuff firmly.

Rnd 18: Decrease around: 6 sc.

Rnd 19: (Skip next sc, slip st in next sc) around; finish off.

HEAD

With Lt Grey, ch 3 **loosely**; being careful not to twist ch, join with slip st to form a ring.

Rnd 1 (Right side): Ch 1, 2 sc in each ch around; do **not** join, place marker: 6 sc.

Instructions continued on page 12.

Rnd 2: 2 Sc in each sc around: 12 sc.

Rnd 3: (Sc in next sc, 2 sc in next sc) around: 18 sc.

Rnd 4: (Sc in next 2 sc, 2 sc in next sc) around: 24 sc.

Rnd 5: (Sc in next 3 sc, 2 sc in next sc) around: 30 sc.

Rnds 6-8: Sc in each sc around.

Rnd 9: (Sc in next 3 sc, decrease) around: 24 sc.

Rnd 10: (Sc in next 2 sc, decrease) around: 18 sc.

Rnd 11: Sc in each sc around; slip st in next sc, finish off leaving a long end for sewing.

Stuff firmly and sew Head to Body.

EAR (Make 2)
With Lt Grey, ch 9 **loosely**.

Row 1 (Right side)**:** Sc in second ch from hook and in each ch across: 8 sc.

Rows 2 and 3: Ch 1, turn; 2 sc in first sc, sc in each sc across to last sc, 2 sc in last sc: 12 sc.

Row 4: Ch 1, turn; sc in each sc across.

Rows 5 and 6: Ch 1, turn; decrease, sc in each sc across to last 2 sc, decrease: 8 sc.

Edging: Ch 1, turn; sc in each st and in end of each row around entire piece; join with slip st to first sc, finish off leaving a long end for sewing.

Sew Ears to Head.

TRUNK
With Lt Grey, ch 3 **loosely**; being careful not to twist ch, join with slip st to form a ring.

Rnd 1 (Right side)**:** Ch 1, 2 sc in each ch around; join with slip st to Back Loop Only of first sc *(Fig. 2, page 15)*: 6 sc.

Rnd 2: Ch 1, sc in Back Loop Only of same st and each sc around; do **not** join, place marker.

Note: Every few rounds, stuff firmly.

Rnds 3-6: Sc in both loops of each sc around.

Rnd 7: Sc in next 3 sc, 2 sc in next sc, sc in next 2 sc: 7 sc.

Rnd 8: 2 Sc in next sc, sc in next 6 sc: 8 sc.

Rnds 9-11: Sc in each sc around.

Rnd 12: Sc in next 5 sc, 2 sc in next sc, sc in next 2 sc: 9 sc.

Rnd 13: Sc in next sc, 2 sc in next sc, sc in next 7 sc: 10 sc.

Rnds 14-16: Sc in each sc around; at end of Rnd 16, slip st in next sc, finish off leaving a long end for sewing.

Flatten Rnd 16 and sew Trunk to Head.

LEG (Make 4)
With Lt Grey, ch 3 **loosely**; being careful not to twist ch, join with slip st to form a ring.

Rnd 1 (Right side)**:** Ch 1, 2 sc in each ch around; do **not** join, place marker: 6 sc.

Rnd 2: 2 Sc in each sc around; slip st in Back Loop Only of next sc: 12 sc.

Rnd 3: Ch 1, sc in Back Loop Only of same st and each sc around.

Rnds 4-6: Sc in both loops of each sc around.

Rnd 7: (Sc in next 5 sc, 2 sc in next sc) twice: 14 sc.

Rnd 8: Sc in each sc around.

Note: Begin working in rows.

Row 1: Sc in next 8 sc, leave remaining 6 sc unworked.

Row 2: Ch 1, turn; decrease, sc in next 4 sc, decrease: 6 sc.

Row 3: Ch 1, turn; decrease, sc in next 2 sc, decrease: 4 sc.

Row 4: Ch 1, turn; decrease twice; finish off leaving a long end for sewing.

Stuff firmly and sew Legs to Body.

TAIL
Row 1: With Lt Grey, ch 6 **loosely**; slip st in second ch from hook and in each ch across; finish off leaving a long end for sewing.

Sew Tail to Body.

Cut two 8" (20.5 cm) strands of Lt Grey. Hold strands together and draw through slip st at end of Tail; tie ends in a knot. Trim as desired.

Add features as desired. •

• ALLIGATOR •
Green - 37 yards (34 meters)

BODY AND HEAD

Rnd 1 (Right side): With Green, ch 2, 4 sc in second ch from hook; do **not** join, place marker **(see Markers, page 15)**.

Rnd 2: Sc in each sc around.

Rnd 3: (Sc in next sc, 2 sc in next sc) twice: 6 sc.

Rnds 4 and 5: Sc in each sc around.

Rnd 6: (Sc in next 2 sc, 2 sc in next sc) twice: 8 sc.

Rnds 7-12: Sc in each sc around.

Rnd 13: (Sc in next 3 sc, 2 sc in next sc) twice: 10 sc.

Rnds 14 and 15: Sc in each sc around.

Rnd 16: (Sc in next 4 sc, 2 sc in next sc) twice: 12 sc.

Rnd 17: (Sc in next 2 sc, 2 sc in next sc) around: 16 sc.

Rnds 18-23: Sc in each sc around.

Rnd 24: Decrease around **(see Decrease, page 15)**: 8 sc.

Stuff firmly.

Rnd 25: (Sc in next 2 sc, decrease) twice: 6 sc.

Rnd 26: 2 Sc in each sc around: 12 sc.

Rnd 27: Sc in each sc around.

Rnd 28: Sc in next sc, 2 dc in each of next 4 sc, sc in next 7 sc: 16 sts.

Rnd 29: Sc in next sc, decrease 4 times, sc in next 7 sc; do **not** finish off: 12 sc.

Stuff firmly.

UPPER JAW
Row 1: Ch 1, do **not** turn; sc in next 6 sc, leave remaining 6 sc unworked.

Row 2: Ch 1, turn; decrease, sc in next 2 sc, decrease: 4 sc.

Row 3: Ch 1, turn; decrease, sc in last 2 sc: 3 sc.

Row 4: Ch 1, turn; sc in each sc across.

Row 5: Ch 1, turn; sc in first sc, decrease; finish off.

LOWER JAW
Row 1: With **right** side facing, join Green with slip st in first unworked sc on Rnd 29; ch 1, sc in same st and in last 5 sc: 6 sc.

Complete same as Upper Jaw.

Sew Upper and Lower Jaws together stuffing firmly before closing.

LEG (Make 4)
With Green, ch 3 **loosely**; being careful not to twist ch, join with slip st to form a ring.

Rnd 1 (Right side): Ch 1, 2 sc in each ch around; do **not** join, place marker: 6 sc.

Rnd 2: 2 Sc in each of next 4 sc, sc in next 2 sc: 10 sc.

Rnd 3: Decrease 4 times, sc in next 2 sc: 6 sc.

Rnd 4: Sc in each sc around; slip st in next sc, finish off leaving a long end for sewing.

Stuff firmly and sew Legs to Body.

RIDGES
SHORT
Row 1: With Green, (ch 2, slip st in second ch from hook) 12 times; finish off leaving a long end for sewing.

Beginning at Rnd 7 and ending at Rnd 22, sew straight edge of Short Ridge to center back of Body.

LONG (Make 2)
Row 1: With Green, (ch 2, slip st in second ch from hook) 19 times; finish off leaving a long end for sewing.

Beginning at Rnd 2 and ending at Rnd 29, sew straight edge of one Long Ridge on each side of Short Ridge.

Add features as desired. •

• GENERAL INSTRUCTIONS •

ABBREVIATIONS

ch(s)	chain(s)
cm	centimeters
dc	double crochet(s)
mm	millimeters
Rnd(s)	Round(s)
sc	single crochet(s)
st(s)	stitch(es)
YO	yarn over

★ — work instructions following ★ as many **more** times as indicated in addition to the first time.

( ) — work enclosed instructions **as many** times as specified by the number immediately following **or** work all enclosed instructions in the stitch or space indicated **or** contains explanatory remarks.

colon (:) — the number(s) given after a colon at the end of a row or round denote(s) the number of stitches you should have on that row or round.

CROCHET TERMINOLOGY

UNITED STATES		INTERNATIONAL
slip stitch (slip st)	=	single crochet (sc)
single crochet (sc)	=	double crochet (dc)
half double crochet (hdc)	=	half treble crochet (htr)
double crochet (dc)	=	treble crochet (tr)
treble crochet (tr)	=	double treble crochet (dtr)
double treble crochet (dtr)	=	triple treble crochet (ttr)
triple treble crochet (tr tr)	=	quadruple treble crochet (qtr)
skip	=	miss

Yarn Weight Symbol & Names	LACE 0	SUPER FINE 1	FINE 2	LIGHT 3	MEDIUM 4	BULKY 5	SUPER BULKY 6
Type of Yarns in Category	Fingering, 10-count crochet thread	Sock, Fingering Baby	Sport, Baby	DK, Light Worsted	Worsted, Afghan, Aran	Chunky, Craft, Rug	Bulky, Roving
Crochet Gauge* Ranges in Single Crochet to 4" (10 cm)	32-42 double crochets**	21-32 sts	16-20 sts	12-17 sts	11-14 sts	8-11 sts	5-9 sts
Advised Hook Size Range	Steel*** 6,7,8 Regular hook B-1	B-1 to E-4	E-4 to 7	7 to I-9	I-9 to K-10.5	K-10.5 to M-13	M-13 and larger

*GUIDELINES ONLY: The chart above reflects the most commonly used gauges and hook sizes for specific yarn categories.

** Lace weight yarns are usually crocheted on larger-size hooks to create lacy openwork patterns. Accordingly, a gauge range is difficult to determine. Always follow the gauge stated in your pattern.

*** Steel crochet hooks are sized differently from regular hooks–the higher the number the smaller the hook, which is the reverse of regular hook sizing.

CROCHET HOOKS												
U.S.	B-1	C-2	D-3	E-4	F-5	G-6	H-8	I-9	J-10	K-10½	N	P	Q
Metric - mm	2.25	2.75	3.25	3.5	3.75	4	5	5.5	6	6.5	9	10	15

■□□□ **BEGINNER**	Projects for first-time crocheters using basic stitches. Minimal shaping.
■■□□ **EASY**	Projects using yarn with basic stitches, repetitive stitch patterns, simple color changes, and simple shaping and finishing.
■■■□ **INTERMEDIATE**	Projects using a variety of techniques, such as basic lace patterns or color patterns, mid-level shaping and finishing.
■■■■ **EXPERIENCED**	Projects with intricate stitch patterns, techniques and dimension, such as non-repeating patterns, multi-color techniques, fine threads, small hooks, detailed shaping and refined finishing.

GAUGE

The following instructions are written for Medium Weight Yarn and that is what we used for our animals but if that is not handy, use Fine Weight Yarn - doubled. Gauge doesn't really matter that much; your animals can certainly be a little bigger, or smaller, without changing the overall effect.

MARKERS

Markers are used to help distinguish the beginning of each round being worked. Place a 2" (5 cm) scrap piece of yarn before the first stitch of each round, moving marker after each round is complete.

DECREASE

Pull up a loop in each of next 2 sts, YO and draw through all 3 loops on hook (**counts as one sc**).

CHANGING COLORS

Work the last stitch to within one step of completion, hook new yarn **(Fig. 1)** and draw through all loops on hook. Cut old yarn and work over both ends, unless otherwise specified.

Fig. 1

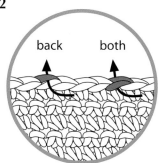

BACK LOOP ONLY

Work only in loop(s) indicated by arrow **(Fig. 2)**.

Fig. 2

FREE LOOPS

After working in Back Loops Only on a round, there will be a ridge of unused loops. These are called the free loops. Later, when instructed to work in the free loops of the same round, work in these loops **(Fig. 3a)**.
When instructed to work in free loops of a chain, work in loop indicated by arrow **(Fig. 3b)**.

Fig. 3a

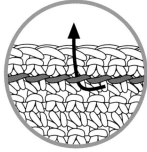

Fig. 3b

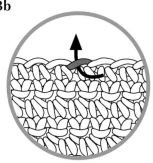

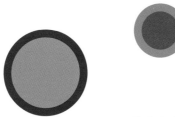

• YARN INFORMATION •

Each Animal in this leaflet was made using Red Heart® Classic™, a Medium Weight Yarn. Any brand of Medium Weight Yarn may be used.

For your convenience, listed below are the colors used to create our photography models.

White - #1 White
Black - #12 Black
Lt Orange - #245 Orange
Orange - #254 Pumpkin
Tan - #334 Tan
Brown - #365 Coffee

Grey - #401 Nickel
Lt Grey - #412 Silver
Gold - #645 Honey Gold
Green - #686 Paddy Green
Rust - #914 Country Red

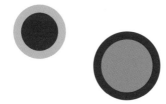

We have made every effort to ensure that these instructions are accurate and complete. We cannot, however, be responsible for human error, typographical mistakes, or variations in individual work.

Animals made and instructions tested by Joan Beebe.

Production Team: Writer/Technical Editor - Linda Daley; Editorial Writer - Susan McManus Johnson; Senior Graphic Artist - Lora Puls; Graphic Artists - Amy Temple and Janie Wright; Photo Stylist - Sondra Daniel; and Photographer - Ken West.

For digital downloads of Leisure Arts' best-selling designs,
visit http://www.leisureartslibrary.com